THE RIDDLE
IN THE TALE

THE RIDDLE IN THE TALE

RIDDLES AND RIDDLE FOLK TALES

TAFFY THOMAS MBE

ILLUSTRATED BY
STEVEN GREGG

The History Press

For storytellers, story listeners,
story readers and riddle lovers,
Wherever you are!

LONDON BOROUGH OF WANDSWORTH	
9030 00005 8984 2	
Askews & Holts	01-Mar-2018
398.6	£9.99
	WW17022218

First published 2017

The History Press
The Mill, Brimscombe Port
Stroud, Gloucestershire, GL5 2QG
www.thehistorypress.co.uk

British Library Cataloguing in Publication Data.
A catalogue record for this book is available from the British Library.

ISBN 978 0 7509 8182 8

Typesetting and origination by The History Press
Printed in Great Britain

A Riddle

What strength and force cannot break through,
I with a gentle touch can do.
And many in the street would stand,
Were I not a friend at hand?

Can you solve this riddle to unlock the
riddles and tales in this book?

CONTENTS

ABOUT the AUTHOR

Taffy Thomas has been living in the Lake District for well over thirty years. He was the founder of the legendary 1970s folk theatre company Magic Lantern, which used shadow puppets and storytelling to illustrate folk tales. After surviving a major stroke in 1985 he used oral storytelling as speech therapy, which led him to find a new career working as a storyteller.

He set up the Storyteller's Garden and the Northern Centre for Storytelling at Church Stile in Grasmere, Cumbria; he was asked to become patron of the Society for Storytelling and was awarded an MBE for Services to Storytelling and Charity in the Millennium honours list.

In January 2010 he was appointed the first UK Storyteller Laureate at The British Library. He was awarded the Gold Badge, highest honour of the English Folk Dance and Song Society, that same year.

At the 2013 British Awards for Storytelling Excellence (BASE) Taffy received the award for outstanding male storyteller and also the award for outstanding storytelling performance for his piece 'Ancestral Voices'.

More recently he has become patron of 'Open Storytellers', a charity that works to enrich and empower the lives of people marginalised because of learning and communication difficulties; he is also the patron of the East Anglian Storytelling Festival.

About the
Illustrator

The illustrations have been drawn by the Cumbrian artist Steven Gregg. Steven was born and raised in the Lake District and currently lives in Windermere. He studied graphic design at Nottingham Trent University and is now working in freelance illustration.

ACKNOWLEDGEMENTS

The Folk Tale collections of Joseph Jacobs have inspired me to commit my own repertoire to print for future generations. Other literary inspirations include the farmer and author from my adopted Lake District, Beatrix Potter. If you revisit the tale of Squirrel Nutkin you will discover the tiny red mammal is a riddle expert.

It is a fact that this book, and all my previous ones, would not have been realised to this standard were it not for the intelligence and unerring support of Chrissy, my wife, my muse and my best friend.

I also need to thank all the like-minded storytellers, both in the UK and in other parts of the world, who have generously shared their material, their skills and their encouragement. This group range from my Scots traveller mentors to the giant that is Daniel Morden, always hugely enjoyable company and never not an inspiration.

Thanks to illustrator Steven Gregg for continuing to be involved and for the wonderful illustrations he produces for my books.

Special thanks to Britain's favourite wordsmith, Michael Rosen, for finding time in his busy schedule to produce the perfect foreword. A bonus for this author and for you, my readers.

Also thanks to Nicola Guy and her team at The History Press for their patience, support and their commitment to published folk tales.

Lastly, thanks to my granddaughter, Ona, who acted as sounding board for my first draft, giving help and intelligent criticism. Also to all those, both children and adults, who for years have asked when I was going to find the time to produce a book of riddles and riddle folk tales. Well, finally I've found the time. So here it is. Enjoy!

FOREWORD

For all the thrills and wonder we get from films, TV, and online entertainment, our first and last link with each other is with face-to-face storytelling. There's a strange rumour going round that it's dead, that we don't do it any more, that we don't talk to each other any more. It's not true. We not only still talk to each other, still tell each other stories, but we have to. Through telling stories, we make ourselves human: we put ourselves into the world around us. Now of course there are many kinds of stories – anything from a 'You'll never guess what happened to me today...' to the *Odyssey* or *Beowulf* or the *Ramayana*.

Somewhere between these two poles of chat and epic comes 'the tale': the short, edgy, catchy tale that could be true, could happen to you, could have happened to her, could have been about him. There are hundreds of different types in many shapes and sizes: jokes, magical tales, mystery tales, wonder tales, wisdom tales; but at the heart of them all is one crucial thing: when someone tells it, do you listen?

This is where Taffy Thomas comes in. When he tells stories, we listen. Now, this is a book, not a teller of tales – but it's a special kind of book. It's one that cries out for anyone anywhere to take what's written here and tell what you've read to others. It's not stealing. It's what storytellers have been doing for thousands of years. The reason why it's not 'stealing' is that the moment you tell one of Taffy's stories here, you won't tell it in exactly the same way as he has. And that's what this book is for. Yes, it's for you to read, enjoy, think about and wonder. It's for you to guess the riddles, admire the way the characters get out of the tricky situations they find themselves in, but it's also a book about passing things on, keeping the tradition alive. You'll see at the beginning of the stories, Taffy often says where and how he got hold of the story in the first place. He's probably telling the truth ...

... but what if he wasn't? What if you thought you'd like to tell one of the stories in this book? You could say you read it in Taffy Thomas's book. Or you could say that you were on the last bus home and there was a man on the bus, sat on his own, singing to himself. You went over to him and asked if he was all right and he told you a story that went like this: 'Once there was a ...'

Well, it could be true. It could have been Taffy ...

Michael Rosen

INTRODUCTION

How to write an introduction to this, my latest book, now that's a riddle in itself. Perhaps I'll go back to basics and keep it simple.

This is my collection of riddles and tales from the oral tradition where each tale is built around a riddle or a collection of riddles.

I think that riddles first came into my life in my childhood in the 1950s. We pulled each other's legs with them in the school playground and read them on tiny slips of paper that spilled from crackers at the Christmas dinner table. My own father gently teased me by asking me how many beans make five? The answer, of course, is 'a bean and a half and half a bean, a bean and a quarter and a quarter bean, a half a bean and a whole bean'. Smiling, he would tell me to add that up; you may choose to do likewise. Annoyingly he was right!

You see, for a riddle to work you need three people: a person who knows it, a person who can answer it, and, for maximum comic effect, a person who gets it wrong. Don't worry, riddles aren't important; but, as Mahatma Gandhi once wrote: 'Everything we do is unimportant, but it's really important we keep doing it.' Eight hundred years before Gandhi wrote that, Leofric, the first bishop of Exeter, deemed them important enough to leave the manuscript for the *Exeter Riddles Book* on his death in 1072.

As a storyteller performing live I regularly tell my audiences I need their brains as well as their ears. Often a riddle can hook an audience and secure instant inclusion and participation. For some of my more archaic riddles, i.e. catkin or harebell, younger readers or listeners may have to work intergenerationally. As a proud grandparent I welcome this communication between young and old, and hope you do too.

What of my sources? As a jobbing storyteller I mainly gather my stories from a living oral tradition, although occasionally I collect from 'guru google', old books or wherever stories are shared. As a fellow patron of the Society for Storytelling once wrote, 'all storytellers are honest thieves'.

I often say 'stories have legs' – so do riddles! As far as my ageing brain allows I include the sources of each tale in their introductions. However, some of this material, gleaned over fifty years, has rolled off my tongue so many times and in so many places that its route to me has been lost in the mists of time. My hope is that this collection is fun for my readers.

But what of the answers? In the tales most answers are revealed as part of the narrative. For the answers to the riddle sections, their answers are there visually in illustrator Steven Gregg's beautiful title pages. If you come across a really tough riddle, the chances are that the one that follows will be much simpler. Read the tales, but share the riddle pages with others. If you are still stuck, the last section in the book is an answers page. But as long as you know how many beans make five, you'll be all right.

Taffy Thomas
The Storyteller's House, Ambleside 2017

The
Riddle Song

Whenever I can, I start my performance set of riddle stories with a version of this song, often sung by my daughter. Wherever we include it, it never fails to please. So it seems right to begin the stories in this book with my version of the song:

I gave my love a cherry without a stone,
I gave my love a chicken without a bone.
I told my love a story without an end,
I gave my love a baby with no crying.

How can there be a cherry without a stone?
How can there be a chicken without a bone?
How can there be a story without an end?
How can there be a baby with no crying?

A cherry when it blossoms it has no stone,
A chicken when it's new-laid it has no bone,
The story that I love you it has no end,
A baby when it's sleeping, there's no crying.

The Stanhope Fairies

In 1991 I was the North
Pennines Storyteller in
Residence. While in this
role, I met a dear friend in
Weardale, a farmer's wife
called Maude Coulthard.
Maude, who is known for
telling jokes at Methodist
teas, passed on this jewel of
a tale, which was of special
interest to me as a collector
of riddles.

In Weardale, County Durham, there are several places where there are strange holes in the ground. The Weardale folk never look into these holes for they know they are fairy holes and, if they peer into the holes and the king of the fairies should see them, he will come at midnight and spirit them away.

There was one young girl, about eight years old, from Eastgate, who was a farmer's daughter. She was desperate to see the fairies at the Eastgate fairy holes. So, one day, when her father and mother were busy on the land, she slipped away and ran towards the fairy holes. As she got closer she could hear the jingling of bells and the clip-clopping of hooves. She sat on the edge of a hole, peered in and saw lots of tiny horses with hooves and bells around the saddle. But the king of the fairies looked up and saw her.

The girl jumped up in terror and ran back to the farm to tell her father what she had done. He called her a silly little goose and told her that the king of the fairies would come at midnight and spirit her away unless she went to bed really early and kept completely silent so that the fairies did not find her.

That night, at six o' clock, the father shut all the chickens and ducks in a shed so there was no clucking and quacking. He stopped all the clocks in the house so there was no tick-ticking and the whole family retired to bed early.

At midnight, the farmer heard the jingling of bells and the clip-clopping of hooves. Knowing it would be the approaching fairies, he kept completely silent. However, he had forgotten that his daughter had a pet dog that slept beside her bed. The dog pricked up its ears and, hearing the jingling of bells and the clip-clopping of hooves, let out a sharp bark.

Now the fairies knew which room to go to. They bundled the little girl into a blanket and took her away with them back to the fairy holes.

When the farmer awoke in the morning he was distressed to find his daughter gone. What could he do?

He knew that, in Stanhope, there was a gypsy woman who lived in a beautiful painted caravan. Perhaps, if he visited her, she could help.

So, that very morning, he walked from Eastgate to Stanhope, a distance of some three and a half miles. He approached the caravan and knocked on the wooden half-door. A thin reedy voice bade him enter. He climbed the three steps into the caravan and found the gypsy woman sitting by the stove making clothes pegs. She asked what he wanted and the farmer explained what had happened to his daughter.

The old woman proffered her right hand and told him that, if he crossed her palm with silver, she could help. The farmer put a hand into his pocket, pulled out a £20 note and pressed it into the gypsy's outstretched hand.

The old woman told him that he must go to the fairy holes himself, wearing a sprig of rowan in his hat for good luck. Furthermore, he would have to take with him three presents – but he would have to answer three riddles to find out the nature of these presents. He had to take: a chicken without a bone; a light that couldn't be lit; and a part of an animal's flesh that could be taken without a drop of blood being drawn.

The farmer couldn't immediately answer any of these riddles, but he did know where to find a rowan tree on the fellside. He thanked the old lady and set out to collect his sprig of rowan, for he needed all the luck he could find.

Halfway up the hill he met a tramp who was starving. The tramp begged an apple, a lump of cheese and half a stottie cake from the farmer, and thanking him, offered his help.

The farmer told him that he needed a chicken without a bone. The tramp explained that this was, of course, an egg.

Delighted, the farmer headed towards the chicken shed to collect his egg.

By the chicken house, a kestrel was diving on a blackbird. The farmer shooed the kestrel away, saving the blackbird's life. Gratefully, the blackbird offered his help. So the farmer told the bird that he needed to find a light that didn't have to be lit. The blackbird informed him that this was, of course, a glow-worm.

So off the farmer headed, towards the wood, to trap this insect.

On the edge of the wood, a naughty boy was throwing stones at a rabbit. The farmer sent the boy home to his mother, so saving the rabbit's life. In return for his kind deed, the rabbit offered the farmer help.

The farmer told him that he needed a part of an animal's flesh without a drop of blood being drawn. Immediately, the rabbit explained that, if he climbed Softly Bank, which is the hill from Weardale into Teesdale, the farmer might find a lizard on the rocks. If he pulled the lizard's tail it would come off without a drop of blood being drawn and the lizard would grow a new one.

So the farmer climbed Softly Bank and, indeed, discovered a lizard scampering on the rocks. He tweaked the lizard's tail and it came off in his hand.

Armed with the tail, the insect and the egg, and wearing the sprig of rowan, the farmer set off back to Eastgate to the fairy holes. He presented these gifts to the king of the fairies, who was so delighted that he told the farmer his daughter could return safely with him to the farm.

And the daughter was so pleased to be going home that she promised her parents that she would never slip off again without them knowing her whereabouts.

Filling The House

*I was told this story
over a cup of cocoa on
one of my journeys as
a travelling storyteller.
My storyteller and artist
friends love this tale,
as we all believe that
music, joy and life are at
the heart of all the arts.*

Somewhere in the heart of the countryside lived a farmer and his three children. His wife had died some time before and he had worked hard to bring up his children well and happy. The house was always full of fun even though they all worked very hard. However, his two sons, who were intelligent, hard-working chaps, had only one grumble: that their sister was always dancing and singing when she should have been working. This didn't seem to bother the farmer as it reminded him of how much his wife had loved to fill the house with singing, and it made him happy.

Now the farmer was in the autumn of his years – the time was approaching when he would die. He knew he would soon have to make a will to say which of his three children would inherit the farm.

He went into town and called on the family lawyer. There he made a will stating that the day he was buried, each of his children was to be given a gold coin. They would have to use this coin to fill every room in the farmhouse from the ceiling to the floor. He had always made sure that the house was full of love and joy and he didn't want that to end with his death. But the old farmhouse was enormous and had many rooms. This would be a test to see which of them would run the farm as it had always been. He was safe in the knowledge that he had made his will, and a couple of years later took to his bed and died.

The day after his death, his three children took his coffin to the churchyard and buried him, full of years. After the ceremony, as the family gathered in the farmhouse, the lawyer arrived to read them the will. All three were keen to know who would get to run the farm. The lawyer explained that their father had left this riddle for them to solve:

> Each will have a piece of gold,
> To bring back something that they hold,
> Which taken in through every door,
> Will fill each room from roof to floor.

Indeed, they were each to get a gold coin and they had to buy something to fill every room in the farmhouse from the ceiling to the floor. Whoever could achieve this would inherit the farm.

The first of the intelligent, hard-working sons went out with his gold coin and his horse and cart; he bought every second-hand feather mattress in area. He returned to the farm and dragged the mattresses into the house. Taking his pocket knife, he slit the mattresses open and filled each of the rooms from the ceiling to the floor with feathers. The lawyer checked from room to room. It took so long to walk around the rooms that by the time he came to the last one, the feathers had settled and there was a gap between the top of the feathers and the ceiling. The lawyer told the lad he liked the idea but there was one room that wasn't quite filled, so he had failed in the task.

The second intelligent, hard-working son took a dustpan and brush and swept up all the feathers. He then went out with his gold coin, and returned with a large box: it was a box of candles. He stood a candle in each of the rooms and lit them all. He had filled every room in the house with light. The lawyer checked from room to room. It took so long to walk around the rooms that by the time he came to the last one, the candle had gone out and the room was in darkness. The lawyer told the lad he liked the idea but there was one room that wasn't quite filled, so he had failed in the task.

That left the music-loving daughter. She went out with her gold coin and returned with a small case containing a flute. For days she sat learning to play a tune, much to the annoyance of her brothers who thought she should be helping them. Eventually she called for the lawyer and all the friends and family to come to the house. She opened the door of every room in the house and sat cross-legged in the hall, playing a lively tune. All in the house started to smile and tap their feet; some even started to dance. At the end of her tune she told the lawyer she had filled every room, not once, not twice, but three times. The lawyer was mystified and asked her to explain. She told him firstly she had filled every room in the house with music; secondly, everyone hearing it had started to smile and dance, so she had filled every room with joy; and if you put music and joy together, she told him, you have life – so even at the time of her own father's death, she had filled every room in his house with life.

The lawyer, and even the brothers, were so impressed by her wisdom and spirit that they agreed she should inherit the farm. She was so happy to keep the house full of life that she agreed that they should all inherit the farm and work together as they always had, as long as she could keep on singing, dancing and filling the house with her music. After all the farm was so big there was room for everyone.

Riddles Good Enough To Eat

*These riddles will feed
your brain, and the
answers your belly.*

1 I am a fruit, but as veg. I am sold,
   I am hot but I sound cold ?

2 A neat little man in a bright red coat,
   A stick in his hand and a stone in his
   throat?

3 My skin is red, but pale within,
   Golden specks upon my skin,
   Sometimes sour, sometimes sweet,
   You'll find me growing at your feet?

4 You throw the outside away to cook the
      inside,
   Then you eat the outside and throw the
      inside away?

5 Toss me up as white as snow,
   When I hit the ground I turn to gold?

6 What bird is with you at every meal?

If you need help solving these riddles, take
another look at the title page of this section.

Happy
Jack &
Lazy John

This story came my way some years ago via American storyteller Alice Murphy, who came to visit the Storyteller's Garden to share stories. It is thought to be a story from France.

The village baker, being now quite old, had handed the bakery on to his twin sons, Jack and John. Now Jack and John, although identical in appearance, were very different in character. Jack was never without a smile on his face and was known to all as Happy Jack. He would awake at first light and bake the breakfast bread, whistling as he worked. John, on the other hand, was a lay-a-bed, and when he did get up from his bed, seldom had flour under his fingernails. Despite this John was as clever as he was lazy, and he enjoyed going out and about selling their wares and keeping the accounts in order. However, everyone still called him Lazy John.

Like with all good bakery establishments, once the ovens were lit the most glorious aromas of baking bread spilled out into the streets and the village square.

So it was when one day the king of that land and his entourage, who were in that area on a hunting expedition, were overtaken by the glorious smell of baking bread. The king at that time was in a state of deep depression, doom-laden with affairs of state, and he hoped that the hunt might cheer him. As the aroma from the bakery reached him he halted the entourage and ordered one of his men to fetch him a loaf of the bread to taste. The king's companion returned, followed by Happy Jack clutching one of his best loaves of the batch. Smiling with delight at the prospect of pleasing the king, Happy Jack bowed and presented the loaf to him. Then he stepped back, his face full of joy, and smiled at the king.

The king, who had not smiled in quite some time, was irritated by Jack seeming not to have a care in the world, and asked him if he was always so happy. Jack replied that he couldn't remember ever knowing a sad day, and was happy all the time.

The king retorted that everyone should encounter some sadness in their life, as it was the way of things. To show Jack that he was no exception to this rule, the king declared that he would set him three riddles, which Jack was to attend the court to answer by noon the very next day. If he failed to do this the bakery would be burned to the ground. For the first time in his life since being an infant Jack was worried and a tear came to his eye.

The first riddle the king asked was:

How much is a king worth?

The second:

What is it that a king needs,
A poor man already has,
But if a man ate it he would die?

Lastly, the king told him that the third riddle would be for Jack to tell him what he, the king, was thinking at the very moment that Jack stood before him the next day.

With this, the king turned his horse and, followed by the entourage, rode off.

Happy Jack stood for a moment watching them ride away and then despondently turned to go back into the bakery. As he went through the door Lazy John had just got up from his bed and, seeing his brother walk in without any smile on his face and with a tear in his eye, asked him what on earth was the matter.

Jack told his brother all that had taken place while he had still been sleeping. He told him all about the riddles and the terrible consequence if he failed to solve them.

Lazy John, who was the cleverest of men, told his brother not to worry and that if Jack let him go in his place then he could answer the riddles and all would be well.

Jack began to feel better, for didn't his brother always know the answer to any question, and didn't his brother always look after him so well that he himself had no worries in the world?

The following day Lazy John arose much earlier than usual and began his journey to the court of the king. When the sun was high in the sky he entered the court room and was taken before the king, who immediately demanded of the young man standing before him if he had the answers to his riddles.

The king confidently set about asking him the riddles, first asking what a king was worth.

Lazy John replied that the greatest man who ever set foot on this earth was sold for thirty pieces of silver and even a king must be worth at least one piece less. So the answer was twenty-nine pieces of silver.

The king seemed surprised at the wisdom of the answer and quickly asked him the second riddle: what a king needs, a poor man already has, and if a man were to eat it he would die. After a short pause Lazy John told the king that the answer was nothing: for a king needs nothing, a poor man has nothing and if a man eats nothing he will die.

The king conceded that this was indeed the answer, but added that unless Lazy John could guess what he was thinking at that very moment then the bakery would burn to the ground. Undaunted, Lazy John told the king that he was thinking that it was Happy Jack in front of him answering his riddles, but that it was not as he thought, for he was in fact Lazy John, Jack's identical twin brother.

Everyone gasped and waited for the king's reaction.

Then, realising he had been outwitted, for the first time in many months the king smiled and then began to laugh. He felt so much better that he told Lazy John that the bakery was spared, and he gave him a handsome reward and sent him home to his brother.

The two brothers kept the bakery for many happy years, and from that day forth they were known as bakers by Royal Appointment.

The Ogre's Riddle

I have been told a version of this story as a Scandinavian tale. However, I treasure my version as it was given to me by a primary school pupil by the walls of Cliffe Castle in Keighley when I was telling stories for her school for their summer picnic.

One fine day the princess was walking towards the castle of her father, the king. As she got close to the castle drawbridge, the ground started to tremble and shake. She began to run as fast as she could towards the castle when the earth cracked open and out jumped a fearsome ogre. The ogre roared so loudly that she stopped in her tracks, and the ogre seized her by the hair and dragged her up the hill towards his house hidden high in the fells. When they entered the gate he took her to the big wooden door of his dungeon and threw her in.

The ogre stood over her menacingly. He snarled at her that he had some bad news … and some worse news! The bad news was that she was his prisoner, and the worse news was that if she couldn't solve his riddle, she'd be his prisoner for the rest of her days. On hearing this she wasn't quite so scared; she had heard about this ogre who liked to play tricks on people to amuse himself, and knew that his intentions were known to be fair. He just loved to outwit people and show his superiority. However, she was a smart lass, she enjoyed riddles, and was rather good at solving them.

Defiantly, she asked for the riddle. The ogre told her that when he returned the following morning, she would have to give him:

> A shiny red box without a lid,
> And deep inside a star is hid.

Sitting on the cold stone floor, the princess looked around the cell in desperation; it was completely empty. Digging deep into her mind, she realised a box can be any shape or any weight as long as it can contain things. She thought of her round jewellery box and her grandmother's pill box. Time to explore. The princess stood up and walked to the far end of her cell; there was a barred window. On the other side of the bars a tree was growing. It had but one branch, and rocking gently on the branch of the tree was one shiny red apple. The princess realised that apples contained pips, so it was in fact a box of seeds, and didn't have a lid! Yes, it had to be a shiny red box. The princess was sure she had the answer, but she couldn't reach the apple. What could she do? She looked at the tree to think of ways she might get the branch to bend towards the window with bars. 'If only you could help me, apple tree,' she said to herself.

Then, magically, something wonderful happened: the tree leaned forward so she could reach through the bars and pick the apple. She realised that she was holding her shiny red box without a lid. Then she thought, 'deep inside a star is hid'. What could that mean? She hoped the following day would take care of that and, exhausted, she curled up in the corner and drifted off to sleep, clutching the apple.

With the first light of morning, the ground started to tremble and shake. The wooden door was flung open and in leapt the ogre.

Sensing triumph, the ogre asked the princess if she'd managed to solve the riddle. With quiet confidence, the princess handed him the apple, pointing out that it was shiny red, a box of pips, and didn't have a lid. Testily, the ogre said that she still hadn't solved the second part of his riddle: 'but deep inside a star is hid'.

The princess fondly remembered times that she'd helped the cook in the castle kitchen prepare apples for her favourite puddings. With a mixture of memory and imagination, she pictured the centre of the apple. She asked the ogre to lend her his knife for a moment. Now sensing defeat, the ogre could only hand her the knife. Carefully, the princess held the apple on its side on a stone: she cut the apple in half across its widest point. Looking at the faces of the two halves, she noted delightedly that where the core had been cut in half and the seeds grew, they formed a star shape. She handed one of the halves to the ogre to show that she had solved his riddle. After looking at it, the ogre knew that he himself had been outwitted.

He told the princess she had been so clever in solving the riddle she could go free, and – as we all know – the princess has lived happily after.

Outwitting
The Devil

A maid and a schoolmaster trade riddles with 'Old Nick', 'Old Scratch', the devil himself. First the tale of the maid in the form of a ballad, followed by the schoolmaster's encounter in the form of a folk tale.

A Riddle Ballad

Riddles have been around for a long time and sometimes appeared in ballad form. The following ballad is one of the oldest in the English language, appearing in the great Child ballad collection as No. 1. The oldest version found was from about 1450.

The story in the ballad is of a meeting between the 'foul fende' and a 'mayd' who has to save herself by answering his questions.

The Devil and the Maid

If you can't answer my questions nine,
Sing ninety-nine and ninety,
Oh you're not God's, you're one of mine,
And the crow flies over the white oak tree.

Oh what is higher than the tree?
Sing ninety-nine and ninety,
And what is deeper than the sea?
And the crow flies over the white oak tree.

Oh heaven is higher than a tree,
Sing ninety-nine and ninety,
And love is deeper than the sea,
And the crow flies over the white oak tree.

Oh what is whiter than the milk?
Sing ninety-nine and ninety,
And what is softer than the silk?
And the crow flies over the white oak tree.

Oh snow is whiter than the milk,
Sing ninety-nine and ninety,
And down is softer than the silk,
And the crow flies over the white oak tree.

Oh what is louder than the horn?
Sing ninety-nine and ninety,
And what is sharper than the thorn?
And the crow flies over the white oak tree.

Oh thunder's louder than the horn,
Sing ninety-nine and ninety,
And hunger's sharper than the thorn,
And the crow flies over the white oak tree.

Oh what is heavier than the lead?
Sing ninety-nine and ninety,
And what is better than the bread?
And the crow flies over the white oak tree.

Oh grief is heavier than the lead,
Sing ninety-nine and ninety,
God's blessing better than the bread,
And the crow flies over the white oak tree.

Oh what is greener than the grass?
Sing ninety-nine and ninety,
And what is worse than man e'er was?
And the crow flies over the white oak tree.

Oh poison's greener than the grass,
Sing ninety-nine and ninety,
And the devil's worse than man e'er was,
And the crow flies over the white oak tree.

Now you have answered riddles nine,
Sing ninety-nine and ninety,
You are God's and can ne'er be mine,
And the crow flies over the white oak tree.

And as she had revealed his name,
Sing ninety-nine and ninety,
He flew away in blazing flame,
And the crow flies over the white oak tree.

The Schoolmaster and the Devil

There was a time when the devil was prowling the earth looking for mischief, when he came upon the little Lancashire village of Cockerham. He was so taken by the little stone houses and sandy church that looked out over the flats that he decided this would be a perfect place for his pranks. So he took up residence in the churchyard itself and set about tormenting all of the locals, so that they were even scared to cross the graveyard path to church or school. As if that wasn't enough, as soon as darkness came he would rattle their windows and doors and drop pebbles down their chimneys. Even the animals howled and shook with fear. This went on as the days became weeks and the weeks became months. Something had to be done. At last a group of villagers were sent to see the village schoolmaster and ask his help to rid them of their tormentor.

The schoolmaster thanked them for their faith in his wisdom, although, as a humble man, he himself doubted his own ability to conquer such a strong dark force. The villagers, being in such terror, implored him to at least try. Seeing their distress, he decided that he must accept the challenge. In relief the villagers sent up three hearty cheers, and in his hiding place among the gravestones the devil wondered what was going on.

He didn't have to wonder long, for as the villagers left the schoolmaster reached for his largest bible, and clearing a space in front of his desk, summoned up the devil.

The schoolroom seemed very quiet when suddenly there was an ear-shattering shriek and a blinding light, followed by a sulphurous smell, and there before the desk stood the devil himself.

In terror the schoolmaster reached towards the bible. As he did the devil spoke to him.

He scorned the schoolmaster for being so fearful, and told him that as he loved a challenge he would give him a sporting chance. The schoolmaster was to set him three riddles and to make them as difficult as he pleased. If the schoolmaster outwitted the devil, then Cockerham would be left in peace. However, if the devil succeeded, the soul of the schoolmaster would belong to him. Then the devil asked for the first riddle.

In despair the schoolmaster turned to look out of the window and saw the mist on the hawthorn hedges. Having an idea, he asked the devil how many raindrops there were on the hedges of Cockerham. Almost before he had finished his question the devil had vanished and re-appeared with an answer. The schoolmaster thought how in his haste he had wasted one of his chances, for he could never disprove the answer he had been given. In desperation he asked his second riddle.

How many cornstalks were in the fields of Cockerham? In the twinkling of an eye the devil vanished and re-appeared with his answer. Again the schoolmaster realised he'd wasted yet another chance, as how could he ever tell if the answers were right or wrong?

The devil reminded him he only had one more chance or both he and Cockerham would be lost. Again the schoolmaster looked out for inspiration and saw the salt flats in the distance. An idea came to him. He asked the devil if it were possible to weave a rope of sand and then wash it in the water.

The devil shot out of the room to solve the task. He tried to weave the sand. Again and again and again he tried. Then he realised that even if he had succeeded in his task he would never be able to wash a rope of sand. He was so incensed that the schoolmaster had outwitted him that he returned to the schoolroom in a rage to tell the schoolmaster that his soul was saved, as was the village. Then, breaking neither door nor window, he leapt up on to the church tower from where he jumped down to Pilling Bridge and then disappeared, never to be seen again. But the hoof print he left can still be seen to this day. The villagers were so proud of the schoolmaster's courage and wit that they vowed never to let the story be forgotten, and it is still told to this day.

In The Storyteller's Garden Riddles Grow

1   I have a black eye and golden hair,
    I grow towards my namesake, high in the air?

2   Old and wise, yet young I may be,
    Drink twice from the riches you gain
        from me?

3   My first is in branch and also in tree,
    My second in pond, but never in sea,
    My third is in water, but not in stream,
    My fourth is in orange, but never in green,
    My last is in end and in answer as well,
    My whole can be seen growing high on the
        fell.
    Down in the vale it overlooks ditches,
    When grown by your gate can protect you
        from witches?

4   First I'm green, then I'm brown,
    When the wind blows, I fall down?

5   Mouse-chaser, closer than friend,
    Wind-dancer, on the bough's end?

6   My first is a creature that frolics in March,
    My second a sound in school or in church,
    Beneath the hedge and above the ground,
    These blue beauties make no sound?

If you need help solving these riddles, take
another look at the title page of this section.

The
Riddle Fish

*I found this story in one of
Joseph Jacob's collections
as 'The stars in the sky'.
In my respectful hands
the title has changed and
several of my favourite
riddles have found a home
in the tale.*

Once upon a time, when the birds drank wine and monkeys chewed tobacco, a mother was tucking her little girl into bed at night when the little girl asked for a bedtime riddle. Her mother, looking out of the window into the night sky, asked her this:

> At sea I am half right,
> With my friends gathered round me,
> You'll see me at night.

The little girl delightedly answered 'the stars', for, as everyone knew, it was her favourite riddle. She had always longed to reach the stars when she saw them shining on clear nights, and had even asked her mother if she could reach them for her. Her mother would tell her that could never be, but she would still fall asleep thinking how happy she would be if she could only reach them.

One day she set off all by herself to find them. By and by she came to the millpond. She looked in to the pond and asked if it had seen the stars in the sky, as she was trying to find them. The pond told her that they often came and play in its water, and if she jumped in she might catch them. So the little girl jumped in and she swam and she swam and she swam but she couldn't find them.

So she went on until she came to a little brook and she asked the brook if it had seen the stars in the sky, as she was trying to find them. The brook told her that the stars often came down and played in the dew on its banks and if she paddled along she might find them. So she paddled and she paddled and she paddled but still she could not find them.

Eventually she came to a meadow and as she looked among the buttercups and daisies she saw the fairies dancing. She asked them if they knew where she might find the stars in the sky. The fairies told her that they often shone in the grass at their feet and if she danced with them perhaps she might find them. So she danced and she danced and she danced but still she did not find them.

Soon she was so tired that she just sat down and cried. She told the fairies that she had swum, she had paddled and she had danced and if the fairies couldn't help her then no-one could.

The fairies whispered to each other and then told her that if she would not turn back then she must journey on and find four legs, and ask four legs to carry two legs to no legs at all; and no legs at all to carry her to the stair with no steps; and if she should climb the stair with no steps then she might be among the stars in the sky.

As the little girl got to the far end of the bank she saw that she was at the edge of a forest. There she saw a horse tied to a tree. She went up to the horse and asked if he could help her to find the stars in the sky. The horse said he knew nothing of the stars in the sky and that his job was only to do the bidding of the fairies. The little girl who loved riddles realised that he must be 'four legs' and that she herself must be 'two legs'. She told him that it was the fairies who had told her to find 'four legs' to carry her to 'no legs at all', who would help her to find the stars in the sky. The horse told her that in that case he would do as they bid, and told her to untie him and jump on his back. So the little girl did as she was told and was soon speeding through the forest clinging to his mane.

At the far side of the forest the horse came to a stop, and there before them was the edge of the sea. He told the little girl to dismount as he had come as far as he could go and had done the fairies' bidding. She asked him where 'no legs' could be, and he told her to be patient and wait. Then he sped back through the forest.

A short time later the the water started to ripple and splash and a large, strange, magical fish appeared at the water's edge. The little girl quickly realised that this must indeed be 'no legs'. She asked the fish if could carry her to the stair with no steps, and the fish replied that it could only do the fairies' bidding. She told the fish that it was indeed the fairies who had sent her to ask 'no legs' to carry her to the stair with no steps so that she might find the stars in the sky. The fish told her that in that case it would do as they bid and she could climb on its back.

She held tight to a fin as it was so slippery on the fish's back. As they swam across the wide sea she saw a curve of bright coloured lights, and the fish told her that she would only know what the stair without steps was if she could answer its riddle:

You'll find me where the rains do dwell;
I also follow the sun as well.

As she looked at the coloured lights she realised the answer and told the fish that, of course, it was the rainbow. The fish flipped its tail and sped towards the bottom of the rainbow. It told her that now she must climb the 'stair with no steps' and it must leave her there as it had done the fairies' bidding. So she slid off the fish's back and it turned around and was soon swimming away.

The little girl peered up to the top of the arch and wondered if she could ever get to the top. Feeling very small, she began to climb and climb and climb but still she had not reached the stars in the sky. It was so steep that she seemed to get no nearer to the top. Soon she became giddy from the bright lights and she lost her balance.

Falling, falling, she would still have been falling now if she had not landed with a bump on the floor of her own bedroom and woken to find it was morning.

She never reached the stars in the sky, but she did have the story of her night-long riddle journey to tell.

Racing For The Crown

*I first heard this riddle
tale when telling stories at
storyteller Ben Haggerty's
Crick Crack storytelling
club in the 1980s.
Subsequently pupils from a
Bradford school told me a
version they had heard from
their mullah. Like the horses
in this tale, stories and
riddles have legs!*

Many years ago there was an old king who had two sons. The boys were twins. Keen to treat them equally, the king bought each of them a race-winning stallion. Each horse was seventeen hands. One prince was given a jet black horse and the other a shimmering grey. The two princes loved to race Jet Black and White Lightning every day in the meadow. Some days one prince won and some days the other. To the old king's delight it panned out very evenly. He had chosen the presents for his young sons well.

The king, however, was in the autumn of his years; the time was approaching when he would die. Before he died he had to make a will to say which of his sons would inherit the crown. This would be a difficult choice for any sensitive father. The king decided to leave them a riddle to settle the decision. His will stated that the day he died the two princes were to take the horses to the meadow and race them. The one whose horse came last would be crowned king. Safe in the knowledge he'd fulfilled his duty to ensure the succession, the old king took to his bed and died.

Even in their grief for their dead father the two brothers couldn't help wondering which of them would be proclaimed king. The king's senior adviser, a famed lawyer, told the brothers that the king had left them a riddle to solve in order to settle the matter. They would have to race their horses, something they did most days, but this time the one whose horse came last would be the winner and thus be crowned king. Wondering, the next day the princes saddled Jet Black and White Lightning and led them to the meadow. The old adviser lined them up side by side before standing well out of the way and shouting, 'On your marks, get set, GO.' Neither prince would move hoof nor hair for they knew the one whose horse came last would be the winner. They stayed put as the seconds turned to minutes, as the minutes turned to hours, indeed until it was just turning dark …

What could they do? As they turned to talk between themselves about their dilemma they remembered that the wisest man in the land was an old storyteller with a long white beard who lived in a remote hut on the far side of the forest. When they were children their father had sometimes taken them to visit this man to hear magical tales, an experience children never forget.

Dismounting and tying their steeds to a post, the princes set out to seek the help of the old storyteller. Always a good idea! Traipsing through the wood to find the clearing on the far side, the princes were relieved to see smoke coiling upwards from the chimney of the old hut, the storyteller's hut; at least he was at home to receive them.

The old man had seen them coming and walked out, leaning heavily on a crooked stick, to meet them. He recognised them as the princes and told them he was sorry to hear of their father's death, as the old king had been kind and caring towards his many subjects; even those who, like himself, lived on the very margins of society. He then told them that he hoped that whichever one inherited the crown would be equally kind and compassionate.

The brothers smiled and told him that it was in fact the business of the inheritance that had brought them to him. They explained the riddle of the horses in the king's will. Puzzling for a moment, the old man stroked his long white beard, looked directly at the princes and spoke just two words.

As soon as the princes heard those two words, they thanked the old fellow and, turning, raced back through the forest to the meadow. Leaping on to the backs of White Lightning and Jet Black, they started to ride as fast as the wind. At the end of the race the old adviser crowned the prince whose horse came last.

My riddle for you is merely to ask what were the two words that the old storyteller said to the princes to solve the riddle and make them start the race?

If this leaves you puzzling to distraction, consult the answers section.

Sam &
The Piskie

*This story was inspired by a
tale told by Scots traveller Jess
Smith. In my version the elf
has become a piskie as I have
set the story in Cornwall.
It is in memory of Sam,
a young Cornish lad who
enjoyed listening to stories
and reading my books.*

It was one of those hot, sunny Cornish days when Sam decided to take a walk down to The Leats to splash his face with water and cool down. As he reached the bank and bent down, cupping his hands to collect the water, a strange thing happened. Every time he tried to scoop up the water it just flowed straight out. He kept trying but the same thing just kept happening. Then he heard a voice coming from the opposite bank, shouting at him to stop what he was doing. As he looked over to where the voice was coming from, he was surprised to see a grumpy little man in a green suit, with pointy ears and pointy boots, shaking his fist at him.

The fierce little man asked Sam what he was doing stealing his water. Sam recognised the little man as a piskie; he had heard about them, but never met one before. Politely he answered that he was just taking a splash of water to cool down.

The piskie said this was not allowed as The Leats belonged to the piskies. Sam told the piskie that The Leats belonged to everyone and wondered if it was the piskie who had been playing tricks on him with the water. The piskie retorted that if anyone took any water they would have to pay for it. Sam said he had no money with him but asked if the pesky piskie would accept something else instead.

Now we all know that piskies are mischievous and love to play tricks on people. So, quick as a flash, the piskie told Sam that he would have to solve three riddles as payment for his water. Now Sam, who was getting hot and bothered and very thirsty, thought he would try the riddles to get the better of this mean little man. The piskie told Sam that he must tell him

What belongs to the wood, goes round the wood, but never goes into the wood?

What has been around for millions of years but is never more than one month old?

And the third riddle would be for Sam to tell the piskie what he was thinking at any exact moment.

Sam thought to himself, whoever would know what a piskie was thinking at any moment? But he was determined to have a go, so he accepted the challenge and said he would be back with the answers after he'd had time to think about the riddles. The little man just laughed at him, sat down on the bank and waited.

As Sam thought about the first riddle, he looked towards the edge of the wood on the other side of the field he was standing in. He walked up to the first tree he came to and saw a friendly squirrel scampering up and down. Now the squirrel had seen the piskie teasing Sam and wanted to help. The piskie often teased the squirrel as well and now he wanted to get his own back.

As Sam watched the squirrel, it gnawed off a piece of bark and brought it over to Sam. Realising the squirrel was helping him, he thought that of course on every tree the bark belongs to the wood, goes round the wood, but never goes into the wood. He had his first answer, and thanked the squirrel for its help.

Turning back towards the bank, Sam noticed a cluster of water lilies. Reclining on a leaf, with its head on a pile of duck down, was a frog. Sam thought the frog must have a very lazy life just lying around on his lily pad, looking up at the sky and dreaming. He wondered if the frog lay gazing upwards both day and night, and thought of him lying there gazing up at the moon at night, watching all its different phases. Then he realised that the moon had been around for millions of years, although we have a new one every month. Now he had his second answer.

As he got nearer the bank, he saw the piskie waiting on the other side, but he still needed his third answer. Who could ever know what a piskie was thinking?

Just then Sam heard the hoot of an owl and thought that the owl would know the answer, for owls are the wisest of creatures. Then he realised, of course, an owl is cleverer than any piskie, even though the piskie considered himself the cleverest creature in Cornwall, if not the whole wide world. He had his third answer, for the piskie would be thinking that Sam would never get the answers and so would be thinking he was much more clever than Sam could ever be.

Sam called out to the piskie that he had his answers. Doubting him, the piskie jumped up and challenged him to give him the answers if he could …

Sam confidently told him the answer to the first riddle was bark. The piskie scowled and asked for the second answer. When Sam told him the second answer was the moon the piskie started to go red with rage, but, confident no-one could outwit him, asked for the third answer.

Sam told him that he was thinking that he was the sharpest-witted creature in Cornwall, if not the whole wide world. Realising that he had indeed been outwitted the piskie jumped up and down in a rage until he toppled over into the water. Now Sam could take as much water as he wanted. And from that time he always had a riddle or story to share.

Four Pairs Of Shorts

*The eight riddles in this
section are mini narratives.
Each is too short to be
considered a full riddle tale,
but each, in its own right, is
a neat riddle. I have paired
them so that on each of the
four pages that follow the first
'short' is from another age,
whereas the one that follows it
is a modern one. This shows
that in the age of computers
and soundbites, we hang on to
the folk tales we still need.*

Short 1

Many years ago, on the edge of the town of Giza in Egypt, a large stone cat, the sphinx, stood on the top of a stepped yellow stone ridge. As soon as any traveller passed the great stone beast they were asked a riddle:

> What has four legs in the morning,
> Two legs in the afternoon,
> And three legs in the evening ?

If, as was usual, they failed to answer this riddle, the sphinx leapt on them and crushed them to death.

One day the Greek adventurer Oedipus was passing while on a long journey home. The sphinx challenged the Greek with the riddle and to the beast's amazement Oedipus answered correctly.

The sphinx was so shocked it tumbled off its high perch down to a lower ridge where it remains to this day.

This is the oldest riddle in the world; can you solve it?

Short 2

A beggar had a brother who lived in Spain,
But the brother had no brother,
Please explain?

Short 3

Two fathers and two sons went fishing.
They caught only three fish.
But at the end of the day, they each ate a whole fish for supper.

How is that possible?

Short 4

One day a woman went to the hairdresser's.

The receptionist told her that she had the choice of two stylists, Poppy or Louise.

The client looked over to the two girls.

Poppy looked absolutely immaculate, but Louise looked as if she'd been 'dragged through a hedge backwards'.

Which of the two did she choose, and why?

Short 5

A man rode into town on Friday.

He stayed for two days and two nights

Then he left on Friday.

How is that possible?

Short 6

A young travelling salesman was in love with a young girl from his village. They were completely happy until a handsome young doctor moved in to the village.

He feared the girl's head would be turned. When he had to leave home for a week of work away, he left his lady with a present wrapped in a brown paper bag. As soon as he'd gone the girl looked in the bag and discovered it contained seven apples.

Why did he leave her those?

Short 7

Two legs sat on three legs eating one leg.
Four legs ran in and grabbed one leg.
Two legs picked up three legs and threw it at four legs.

As three legs hit four legs it dropped one leg into a cow pat.

With their heads down two legs and four legs went back in to the house hungry!

Short 8

A policeman walked past a house. He heard a woman scream, 'Don't do it, John!'.

BANG!

He burst open the door and ran in.

The woman lay dead on the floor with a smoking gun next to her. Standing around the corpse were a dustman, a dentist, a doctor and a lawyer, all unknown to the policeman.

The policeman rushed up to the dustman and arrested him.

He was right, but how did he know ?

King James &
The Bishop Of
Worcester

Whereas King John and the Abbot of Canterbury is an ancient, riddle-filled, song ballad, the story that follows is my version of a tale I heard orally from my friend the cultural treasure that is singer and storyteller Ken Langsbury. The story holds firm, but remember the author is a storyteller not a historian. Are you as clever at riddles as the gardener?

More than four hundred years ago James VI of Scotland united two nations by becoming James I of England. The king and a small retinue took the decision to venture south of the border to inspect the extent of his wealth. James and his group of soldiers, courtiers and flunkies broke their journey south at convenient castles like Carlisle, York and Warwick before venturing further towards the south-west. Arriving at the ancient city of Worcester, he reached the stone gateposts of the Bishop of Worcester's palace. On the palace gate was a big brass plate which read, 'Here lives the Independent Bishop of Worcester'. King James didn't much approve of this arrogant boast and demanded to see the bishop immediately. He challenged the bishop to explain his boast.

The bishop told the king he had this sign made because he wanted it to be known that he didn't give way to any man, pauper or prince. The king didn't think much of this and decided to challenge the bishop. He told the wealthy cleric that he would test this arrogance by asking him three riddles.

The first riddle he posed to the bishop was:

How long would it take me to go all around the world?

The second riddle he asked him was:

How much am I worth, down to the last farthing?

Lastly he told the bishop that on their next meeting he would ask the riddle:

What am I thinking at this moment?

Who could ever know what a king is thinking? The bishop looked mystified. The king told him he should come to London, to his new residence at Hampton Court, by the end of the week. If he was unable to correctly answer these riddles he would lose the right to call himself the 'Independent Bishop of Worcester'.

For two days the bishop wandered around his palace looking worried. He couldn't solve one of the riddles, let alone three. On the third day he did the only thing he could think to do: he went for a walk in his extensive gardens. The old gardener, wise from years of living close to the earth, spotted his master with his head down and his brow furrowed and asked if he had a problem that he could help with. The bishop told the gardener that he was fine and to get on with his weeding. Sensitive and loyal, the gardener again asked if there was something worrying the bishop that he could help with. The bishop told him that as he'd been a good and faithful servant for years he would share the problem, or to be more precise the three problems. Listening to the riddles the gardener paused and asked his master if the king knew him well. The bishop told him they had only met once, briefly.

Then the gardener told him that he had a plan. He would dress up in the bishop's clothes the following day and ride to London and face King James to answer the riddles. He knew no fear, but more importantly, he knew the three answers!

The following morning, the gardener dressed in the bishop's best robes and, mounting his master's white horse, rode off to London.

Arriving at Hampton Court his horse was stabled as he was ushered to a large room where King James sat on a throne surrounded by his courtiers, who were already not fond of the new monarch, having found him bullying and brash. The king announced that it was time for the first riddle.

How long will it take me to go all the way around the world?

The old gardener, disguised as the bishop, told the king that if he travelled with the sun it would take him exactly twenty-four hours. The king looked furious, and the bullied courtiers sniggered behind their hands. The king, bloodied but unbowed, tried again, asking him:

How much am I worth to the nearest farthing?

Bravely the gardener answered that as the only man to walk this earth who was worth anything was sold for thirty pieces of silver, by that reckoning, King James was not even worth a farthing. The king looked even more furious, as the courtiers had to bite their hands with pleasure at seeing their cruel master again outwitted.

The king had one more riddle in his …….. that he was sure could never be answered correctly. He asked the old man standing in front of him in the purple robes:

What am I thinking at this moment?

Confidently, the gardener said that the king was thinking that the man facing him and answering his riddles was the Bishop of Worcester, but in fact he was only the bishop's old gardener in disguise.

King James was red with rage as the courtiers finally dared to release a muffled chuckle. In the confusion that followed the old gardener fled for his life. He mounted the white horse, and galloped back to Worcester where he received a bag of gold and grateful thanks from the 'Independent Bishop of Worcester'.

The Greatest Gift

Since I started telling this tale I've come across a Spanish version and also a Turkish version. I think any narrative that poses a dilemma is indeed a riddle story, for what is a dilemma if not a riddle that needs solving?

There were once three brothers who were the best of friends. They had a favourite uncle who always brought them wonderful stories from his travels around the world. He would also, from everywhere he went, bring each of them a present. So the three brothers were always eagerly awaiting his return, to hear magical stories of faraway places, and to know who would receive the next gift.

Now, at that time throughout the kingdom it was proclaimed that the time had come for the king to find a husband for his daughter, the princess. The king was very proud of his daughter and decreed that if he had to give her up, he had to be given something as precious in return. The greatest gift in the world. Many suitors had come with their gifts, but no-one had been successful in convincing the king that theirs was the greatest gift.

Now it happened that the uncle had returned from his latest travels with wonderful stories from exotic lands and the brothers sat and listened to them with wide eyes. Then, as the stories came to an end, the brothers waited excitedly to see what their presents might be.

The uncle handed the eldest brother a mirror. It seemed to the boy that it was just an ordinary plain mirror, and he was disappointed. The uncle looked at him and explained that it was a mirror with magic powers that could make a person that you were thinking about appear within it. The boy looked doubtful, but the uncle told him to think of his father, and sure enough an image of his father working out in the fields appeared in the mirror. The eldest son was delighted with his present.

Next the uncle turned to the middle brother and presented him with a small rolled-up carpet. The brother unrolled the carpet and saw that it had been well-worn and he too was disappointed with his present. The uncle told him to sit on the carpet and think of his favourite place. The brother knelt on the carpet and, amazingly, off it flew out of the window. Within a few minutes it reappeared in front of them all with the middle brother full of excitement. He told them that he had thought of the old willow tree by the river that they often visited to fish. The carpet had taken him there, and when he thought of how he wanted to tell his brothers about it, the carpet had flown back to the very room that they were all in. The middle brother was also delighted with his present.

As the uncle turned to the youngest brother, he smiled. This brother was gentle and trusting and secretly his favourite. The uncle presented him with a beautiful plump lemon and told him that he must trust him that it was a magic fruit that could cure any sickness. Then he told him to use it wisely as it could only be used once. The other brothers smiled. A lemon! They loved their young brother and knew him to be very trusting, but how could he know if it would work?

The next day the uncle left to pursue new travels and adventures and the boys felt sad to see him go. After all, wasn't he such a wise and mystical man, and how happy they were listening to his stories.

When the brothers were left together discussing the presents their uncle had brought, they also talked about the great decree from the palace and the visits of all the noble suitors seeking the hand of the princess. The eldest brother had an idea. If they looked in to the mirror and thought of the palace they could see what was happening there.

As they peered into the mirror they saw the king in a bedchamber, weeping. As they watched they realised that the princess was lying in the bed, surrounded by doctors and looking pale and sick. They realised at once that she must have the terrible fever that had been going around the kingdom, causing much worry and sadness.

The brothers thought that they must try to help. The middle brother knew what to do. He unrolled the carpet and told the others to jump on, and then as he thought of the scene they had witnessed in the mirror, the carpet took off, flew through the window and landed in the bedchamber they had seen in the palace.

The king immediately drew his sword and asked them how they had come to be there. The brothers bowed and told the king of the magic mirror and the flying carpet, and how they had felt compelled to come and help. They told him how the youngest brother had a magic fruit that could cure all sickness.

The youngest son handed his special lemon to the doctors standing around the bed, saying that he believed it would help. The doctors immediately took the lemon and squeezed out the juice and put it to the lips of the princess. As the princess drank, slowly each sip seemed to lessen the fever until she had sipped all of the juice. The princess was able to sit up and hold her hand out to her father, who was overjoyed.

The king called the boys to him and said that they would receive a great reward. He called for his wisest sage, the one who he knew could give the best counsel. The brothers were amazed to see their uncle enter the room and bow to the king. The king asked him what would be the best reward to give the brothers. The wise uncle told the king that if he could solve his riddle he would know the answer to that question.

The king asked to hear the riddle, and this was it:

> The mirror showed someone in need,
> The carpet flew with greatest speed.
> The lemon made the sickness lift,
> But which brother gave the greatest gift?

The king looked puzzled and the princess looked up at him and said that she knew the answer. That the mirror and carpet gifts from the two eldest brothers were indeed great, but the greatest gift, that of life, had come from the youngest brother. For indeed he had given all he had to save her life.

Now the king understood that the youngest brother had given him the greatest gift, that of his daughter's life, and he deserved her hand in marriage even though he was not one of the noble suitors. The uncle just smiled knowingly as the king thanked him for his wisdom.

So the youngest brother and the princess were married and were kind and fair rulers. And the two older brothers were happy for them, and with their mirror and their carpet also had long lives full of adventures.

Of course, without the wisdom in the riddle from the uncle, the king may never have come to make that choice.

A Riddle Gallimaufry

1   Without a bridle or a saddle,
        Across a thing I sit astraddle.
        And those who ride with help of me,
        Though almost blind, are made to see?

2   My coat is wood,
        My nose is dark,
        And where I go I leave my mark?

3   Weight in my belly,
        Trees on my back,
        Nails in my ribs,
        But feet I do lack ?

4   When the horse strokes the cat,
        The wood sings ?

5   Brothers we are two
     And we are sore oppressed.
     In the daytime we are full
     And empty when you rest?

6   The man who made me never kept me.
     The man who bought me never used me.
     The man who used me never saw me?

If you need help solving these riddles, take
another look at the title page.

The Fearsome Giant

This story hails from a land of mountains and valleys, 'the land of my fathers', Wales. It has all the magic of the traditional riddle tale, but with it comes the wisdom that often defines the powerful endurance of traditional stories.

Along, long time ago in a far away land, there was a beautiful kingdom nestled in a peaceful valley surrounded by towering mountains.

There was only one road into the valley, the only way to enter or leave the kingdom. The road passed between the two tallest mountains through a gap created by the waters of a babbling mountain stream. It was a very busy road and often filled with people merrily coming and going. People would come from far and wide to visit this peaceful kingdom.

All seemed well.

One day something terrible happened. At the border of the kingdom, by the side of the one and only road between the two mountains, a fearsome giant set up home. Stories spread quickly, claiming that the giant frightened all the people coming and going along that road through the mountain gap. It was said that the giant would stand and cast his long shadow across the land and his booming voice would thunder:

> Swish, swash, bang, boom.
> I am your nightmare.
> I am your doom!

The people ran away, frightened, and they would tell tales of terrible things the fearsome giant did, how he picked up entire horses and carts with his bare hands and smashed them back down to the ground, or how he would jump up and down and make the earth tremble for miles around, all the time chanting:

> Swish, swash, bang, boom.
> I am your nightmare.
> I am your doom!

The people were so frightened they decided to go to the king and demand that something must be done to rid them of this fearsome giant. Now, the king of this land was a young man, a very young man indeed. In fact, he was still a youth who had only recently inherited the throne. His parents, the old king and queen, had been rulers for a very long time and had been very wise and much loved by the people of the land. However, they had died not long before the fearsome giant had appeared. Of course the young king wanted to prove himself as brave and wise as his parents, but he secretly feared that he just wasn't good enough.

The people demanded that he send out his knights to destroy the giant. The king, being young and uncertain, thought he must do as the people demanded as that would make them happy. So the king called for his four bravest knights. These knights were so brave, they were possibly the bravest knights in all the world and they could always manage to sort every problem that confronted the kingdom. The king was certain they could deal with the giant. He commanded the knights to go forth and drive the fearsome giant out of the land. The people applauded and cheered as the knights set out and they were filled were pride and hope.

Although they were certainly very brave and capable, as the knights became close to where the giant lived they started to become worried. They told each other the terrible stories they had heard about the giant, and they soon realised that not one of them had faced a giant such as this before, they were soon feeling more afraid.

As they reached the mountain gap, the giant saw them coming. He rose to his feet and stood before them. He cast his long shadow over the knights and began to jump up and down. The earth trembled mightily and then his voice thundered:

> Swish, swash, bang, boom.
> I am your nightmare.
> I am your doom!

The horses reared up on their hind legs, dumped the knights on to the road and galloped away with the knights running for their lives behind them.

Well, if the people were scared before, when they saw that the knights had failed they were terrified. They demanded that the king must find another way to rid them of this fierce and terrible giant. The young king did not know what to do. He wished his mother and father were there because they had always seemed to know what to do. He realised that he missed them very much.

As he sat thinking of how he needed their help more than he ever had, he suddenly remembered the wise old hen-wife. She lived at the edge of the forest where he had sometimes hunted with his father. He remembered that his mother trusted her, and he heard people say how much she had helped them. He had never met her but somehow felt that if anyone could help him it would be her. So he decided to ride to the forest to find her and seek her advice.

The young king found a cottage nestled on the edge of the forest and knocked on the door. A thin reedy voice told him to enter. There was an old woman sitting by the fire. He knew it was the hen-wife. She was very old but the young king could sense her wisdom. She had a welcoming smile.

The hen-wife asked how she could help the king. He wondered how she seemed to know who he was, but didn't ask. He anxiously told her all about the fearsome giant and the terrible stories he had heard. The hen-wife listened carefully, and when the king had finished speaking she thought for a long time and finally she spoke. She told him that she would tell him a riddle that, when solved, would answer his problem. However, he needed to ponder the riddle himself and then he would know what to do. This was the riddle:

> If you run from what you do not know,
> It will seem to grow and grow,
> Then it will stand within your way,
> Until its name you learn to say.
> What is it?

And then the hen-wife smiled, wished him luck, and returned to her fire.

As you might imagine, the young king felt a bit confused. He left the cottage and returned to the castle. He thought and thought about the riddle but still didn't know what it all meant. He had wanted her to tell him what to do, but it seemed that he had to figure it out for himself. But he somehow knew that the riddle held the answer.

The people were still calling out for the young king to do something. Yet what was he going to do? He was frightened just thinking about the giant, but he knew he had to be the one who sorted it out. Everyone was depending on him. Then he thought about the riddle of the wise old hen-wife.

> If you run from what you do not know,
> Then it will seem to grow and grow,
> Then it will stand within your way,
> Until its name you learn to say.
> What is it?

The young king made a decision. He decided he could run away no more. Armed with the riddle, he himself would face the giant. He spoke to his people and told them he would fight the giant, and they all stared in disbelief as they watched him mount the royal steed and begin his journey towards the dangerous border.

As the young king approached the border, the fierce giant stood up and towered over him. The giant bared his teeth and growled loudly. The young king was terrified. His royal steed was terrified. So terrified, that the king had trouble controlling him.

The king dismounted and tried to tie his horse to a fence but it reared and chased away towards the town. The young king stood alone before the huge and terrible giant.

The giant jumped up and down and the earth trembled. The giant's voice thundered:

> Swish, swash, bang, boom.
> I am your nightmare.
> I am your doom!

The young king felt a very large knot at the bottom of his stomach and his legs were feeling like jelly. He was scared. The trembling of the earth and the roaring of the giant caused the young king to take several steps backwards. But as he took each step backwards the giant seemed to get bigger and bigger.

He wanted to turn and run away from the huge and terrible giant. But he also wanted to do what a king must do. He stopped himself from running. He took a deep breath. Then he remembered the riddle of the hen-wife:

If you run from what you do not know,
Then it will seem to grow and grow,
Then it will stand within your way,
Until its name you learn to say.

Only then did the king understand the riddle. Not knowing what would happen, he took three great steps towards the giant. As he took the steps, a strange thing happened. The giant seemed to get smaller.

Even though part of him still wanted to run away, he decided to keep on walking towards the giant. With each new step the giant became smaller and smaller in size. The giant jumped up and down but the earth no longer trembled. He tried to roar but what came out was just a whimper and not at all like thunder:

> Swish, swash, bang, boom.
> I am your nightmare.
> I am your doom.

The young king kept on walking right up the giant, who with each step had become no bigger than the king's thumb. He bent down and picked up the tiny giant and stood him on the palm of his hand.

He wondered how the giant could possibly have done all the things the people said he'd done.

The king looked the tiny giant in the eye and said, 'Tell me your name?'

The tiny giant blinked and squeaked, 'My name is FEAR.'

The king now saw the wisdom of the old hen-wife's riddle and knew he had the answer. The thing that had scared him most was fear itself. From that day onwards he became a beloved king who never forgot to face his fears in order to protect his people.

Clever Manka & Princess Rose

The story that follows is an elaborate riddle story known throughout Europe. In England only the final part of the story has survived as a fragment entitled Princess Rose. As Princess Rose is the tale I more commonly tell, I have included both the full tale and the fragment in this collection. Firstly, the big tale.

Once there were two men, one poor and one comfortably rich. The wealthy man, a farmer, lived with his wife, but the poor man, his labourer, was a widower and he lived with his daughter, Manka, who was kind-hearted and wise beyond her years. The two men were one day digging together in a field, and as they tilled the earth the labourer discovered a gold cup. Immediately the farmer started to argue about which of them should have it. The farmer argued that he should have first claim as the valuable cup was buried in his field. The peasant argued that he had found it and been the one to dig it out of the ground. They quarrelled as the seconds became minutes and as the minutes became hours. The only way to settle the dispute was to bring the matter before the judge.

At first the judge, a bright and clever young man, could not work out how to resolve the case. After a period of deep thought he decided the fairest way was to ask both the two men the same riddle, and whoever could answer best would keep the gold cup.

The riddle was this:

> What is the richest thing in the world,
> What is the heaviest thing in the world,
> And what is the sweetest thing in the world?

The farmer went home, and his wife asked him what had happened with the judge. He told her about the riddle and asked for her help. His wife told him she knew all the answers; for the richest thing in the world must be the king; the heaviest thing in the world was, of course, iron; and the sweetest thing in the world was indeed the honey lying in their cask.

The poor peasant, who didn't have a wife to help him, went home to his daughter Manka who, being as we know smart beyond her years, asked why he looked so worried and if she could help him. He told her about the judge's riddle. Listening to the riddle, Manka had some very different answers to the rich man's wife. Manka told her father to go to the judge the next day and tell him that the richest thing was the earth itself because it provides for all; the heaviest thing was sorrow which lies on a man with greater weight than iron; and the sweetest thing was sleep, for sleep could make you forget your worries and give you happy dreams.

The following day the two men were called before the judge and each presented their riddle answers to him. On hearing their answers, the judge immediately presented the cup to the poor man, telling him that his answers were indeed wise so he should win the case. Then he asked if he had solved his riddle by himself or if anybody had helped him. At first the peasant did not want to admit the truth, but being an honest man he told the judge that his young daughter Manka, who was wise and clever beyond her years, had helped him. Intrigued, the judge wished to meet her and asked him to bring her to him the following day.

The next day when Manka and her father arrived, the judge was in the middle of deliberating over another difficult case. A father had died, leaving his two sons the farm. Part of the farm was rich and fertile and the other half of the farm was barren and dry. Whichever way the judge decided, neither of the brothers would be satisfied. The judge greeted Manka and her father, and thought to himself that she was as beautiful as she was wise. He asked her what she would do in deciding the case brought before him. Manka suggested that one brother should divide the land and the other brother should choose which half he would take. On hearing the wisdom of this solution the two brothers left happily and in harmony. The judge complimented Manka for her intelligence and for her beauty. The judge told Manka's father that he was looking to marry and could think of no-one more suited to be his wife than clever Manka. So he asked for her hand in marriage if she would agree. Manka, who really liked the judge, was willing.

The judge, however, was to set Manka one last test to satisfy himself that she was indeed as wise and clever as she seemed, and of course once again it was a riddle. He told her that on their wedding day she should come to him neither clothed nor naked, neither riding or walking, and finally neither with a wedding gift nor without one. When her father heard this he feared they would never be wed. Manka calmly asked her father to go to the town and buy her a fine fishing net and a live pigeon. The following morning, on the day of her wedding, Manka woke up and wrapped herself in the fishing net so that she was neither naked nor dressed. She saddled her goat and her feet touched the ground on either side, so that she was neither walking nor riding. She also clutched the pigeon in her hands as she rode towards the judge's chambers.

As the judge saw her arriving he smiled to himself at the wit of the young girl. As he went out to greet her she presented him with the pigeon as his wedding gift, but as she opened her hands the bird flew away. Delighted, the judge told Manka that they would indeed be married provided that she promised never to interfere with his work and his judgements. If she was ever to break that promise she would be sent home to her father and the marriage would be over. So the judge and Manka were married and for quite some time all was well. Manka, who was kind and good-hearted, became well-liked as the judge's wife. Then one morning something happened ...

Two men arrived at the court, one of whom was leading a foal. They wanted the judge to decide the ownership of the foal. One owned the mare who had given birth to the foal, the other owned the stallion. Both men claimed that the foal was theirs. The judge decided that the foal should be given to the man who owned the stallion, because as a man of wealth and standing in the district he had put forth the most convincing argument.

The less eloquent man, who owned the mare, felt cheated. He had heard that the judge's wife was both wise and kind-hearted, and went to her to seek advice. Manka was reluctant to assist, but feeling that justice had not been done, she told him what he could do to help his case. Manka told the man to cast his fishing nets on the side of the mountain where the judge would be passing that very afternoon after closing the court, and then she told him what to say. The man ran home and immediately did as Manka suggested. As the judge rode past he looked up and saw the man casting his nets; he asked the man why he was doing such a strange thing as he had no chance of catching any fish there. The man shouted back that he had as much chance of catching fish there as a stallion did of giving birth to a foal. The judge laughed and, taking on board the lesson he had been taught, he decided he should reverse his decision and award the foal to the man with the mare. Then he called the man to him and asked him if he had come up with the idea to do this himself or had he been helped? The man tried carefully not to reveal Manka's secret but after much persistence from the judge the man revealed that it was the judge's wife herself who had helped. It was just as the judge had suspected.

Returning home, the judge faced Manka, angrily telling her that she must return to her father as she had broken their wedding promise and now their marriage was over. Manka sadly agreed to leave, and had only one request, to take with her just one thing from their home that she most loved. The judge agreed to her request. Manka had a plan. She had agreed to leave the next day, but as supper arrived Manka slipped a sleeping potion into the judge's wine. Before the meal was over the judge felt incredibly tired and retired to bed where he fell into a deep sleep. Manka then asked their servants to carry the judge's bed containing the judge to her father's house and she followed behind.

The sun was high in the sky when the judge finally awoke. He looked around and was amazed to find himself in a room he did not know. He called for his servants, but none came. Then Manka came running through the door and told him that they were at her father's house. Just as the judge had agreed, all she had done was to bring with her the thing that she loved the most, the judge himself.

The judge smiled and realised that Manka once again had the better of him and was wiser than he could ever be. He said that they should return to their house together, and from that day forth, as Manka was so wise, she should sit beside him in court and they should give judgement together. And so it was done, and from that day all has been just and fair for the people of that district.

The Princess Rose

Once there was a good king who had a daughter, the Princess Rose. The king was old and Princess Rose, who was loyal and loving, stayed home to look after him. But the drums were beating on the border and the good king was called to arms against the young king of the neighbouring kingdom.

The young king was ambitious to conquer new lands and add them to his empire, but was advised that the old king's land was so small that to take in a vast army would not be fair. So he decided to find another way to acquire the kingdom.

He sent the old king a flock of sheep and told him to sell them and then return them to him along with the money he made on the sale. If he did not do this his kingdom would surely be taken from him. The old king was worried, as he knew that his army was no match for that of the young king.

Princess Rose saw the despair on her father's face and determined to help. She was as clever as she was kind and beautiful, and told him that she would have an answer to his problem by the next morning. The next day she told him to have the sheep sheared and then raise the money he needed by selling the wool at market. So the king did as she said, and the following day the sheep and the money were returned to the young king.

When he saw that he was outwitted, the young king sent a message to the old king, asking who had helped him to resolve the problem. For he had been told the old king had been in despair and had no idea how to save his kingdom.

The reply was soon sent to him that the old king was proud to say that the Princess Rose was the one who had been clever enough to know what to do.

The young king was impressed. He wanted to meet Princess Rose and see if she was as clever as her father claimed. He told the old king to bring the princess to his court, but that she was to come neither dressed nor naked, neither walking nor riding and neither bearing a gift nor empty-handed. He also told him that if she succeeded in doing this the old king could keep his kingdom, but if not he would lose both the kingdom and his life.

The old king looked at his daughter anxiously, but she smiled back at him and told him that she was a match for any of the young king's riddles. She sent for a fishing net from the fishermen down on the beach, a donkey and a dove from the dovecot in the palace gardens, saying then she would be ready to meet the young king.

The next day the old king set out with his entourage, and in the middle of them was the princess. As they eventually approached the palace of the young king he emerged to see the Princess Rose riding on a donkey with the fishing net draped around her bare shoulders. She was riding by the gutter of the palace pavements with one foot trailing on the ground, and in her hand she was holding the dove. She rode towards the young king and held out the dove, but as he reached out to take it she let go of it and it flew away.

The young king was impressed at how she had risen to his challenge and declared that he had never met anyone as clever as she. He agreed that as she had solved his riddle her father could indeed walk free. As Princess Rose returned home with her father, he rejoiced in the fact that in her not only did he have a daughter who was loyal and loving, but that she was the sharpest-witted woman in the whole of his kingdom. He thought to himself that 'a son is a son 'til he finds a wife, but a daughter is a daughter for the rest of your life'.

Riddles Grow Out Of The Land

1   What always runs but never walks,
        Often murmurs but never talks,
        Has a mouth but never eats,
        And has a bed but never sleeps?

2   I have six arms,
        I can swallow whole farms,
        And a million can
        Become a man?

3   An ocean that ripples,
        Shimmers and drowns,
        Yet not a drop of water
        Is to be found?

4   I am the keeper
        Of night and day,
        Every step closer to me
        Is one step further away?

5   Rivers without water,
      Forests without trees,
      Deserts without sand,
      And beaches without seas?

6   For time I've given measure,
      For some I've hidden treasure,
      Hard as stone,
      Soft as silk,
      Black as ash,
      White as milk?

7   I've got no wings, but I can fly,
      I've got no voice but I can cry,
      I've got no teeth but I can bite?

If you need help solving these riddles take
another look at the title page of this section.

The Pot
Of Gold

The oldest version of this little gem of a story that I have found seems to be a version in an Italian folk tale. However, my dear friend, American storyteller Dan Keding, told me that his East European grandmother used to tell him a version of it. Perhaps this is just further proof that, as I say, 'stories have legs'.

There was once a farmer who had a fine olive grove. He was very hard-working so the farm was always prosperous under his care. Now, the farmer had three sons who were strong and fit young men, but all of whom had no desire to become farmers, they hated the work. In fact when they got together they were workshy. As farmers would often say, 'A lad is a lad, two lads are half a lad, three lads are no lad at all.' They dreamed of seeking their fortunes or making easy money.

The farmer worried about their future and what would happen when he was no longer there to keep the harvest coming, but with little help from them he had to continue to work very hard. They just said that it was his love and passion and that was what kept him going.

One day, however, the farmer felt that he no longer had the strength and drive to keep the orchard as well as he always had. He felt that the time was approaching when he might die. He called his sons to him and told them that soon the land would be in their hands and that he worried for their survival without the fruits of the olive grove, and for the survival of the farm. He told them to gather near and listen. He told them he had a riddle for them and if they could work it out they would all prosper well without him. Then he told them his riddle.

> Before becoming frail and old,
> In the grove I buried a pot of gold.
> So when your fortune's not at hand,
> You must dig beneath our land.

The sons tried to get him to tell them the whereabouts of the pot of gold. They wanted immediate gain without the work of solving the riddle or digging; but he would say no more.

When the time soon came that the farmer died, the sons thought they might as well set to work to find the pot of gold. Once again they puzzled over the riddle.

> Before becoming frail and old,
> In the grove I buried a pot of gold.
> So when your fortune's not at hand
> You must dig beneath our land.

They had no idea of the hiding place, so they agreed to work in a line from one end of the orchard to the other, digging the soil round the roots and between them. But, alas, no pot of gold was to be found. It seemed that it must have been stolen or that their father's memory had been playing tricks. They were not happy to have done all that work for nothing.

Soon they went back to their old ways, but the money their father had left them had begun to dwindle and the winter became harder.

Then, as the next olive season approached, they saw that the trees bore more fruit than they ever had before. The cultivation they had had from the digging brought so much fruit, of such fine quality, that when the sons sold it they found that it gave them a whole pot of gold.

When they saw how much money had come from the olive grove they thought of their father's riddle.

> Before becoming frail and old,
> In the grove I buried a pot of gold.
> So when your fortune's not at hand,
> You must dig beneath our land.

Now they had the answer; they understood what he had meant about gold being hidden in the grove. They also realised what a wise and caring father he had been and vowed that if they had sons of their own, they would always teach them the value of the gold hidden in the land, and that 'when their fortune would be found, they should search beneath the ground'.

Counting Sheep

In the UK there is a rich tradition of mathematical puzzles and riddles. 'Counting Sheep' came to me via an eight-year-old boy, although I love telling it both in schools and to adults at Lakeland Shepherds' meets.

Deep in Lakeland, there lived an old farmer and his three sons. Their farm was a sheep farm, and boasted a fine flock of Herdwick sheep.

The farmer in this tale was in the autumn of his years. The time was approaching when he would die. He had to make a will to state which of his three sons would inherit the farm and the sheep. The will stated the day he was buried the sheep were to be divided between the three brothers. The oldest was to have half the sheep. The middle brother was to get a third of the sheep, and the youngest brother a ninth. Safe in the knowledge he'd completed his will, the farmer took to his bed and died in his sleep.

The following day, the three brothers took his body to the churchyard and laid him in the ground, full of years. The brothers returned to the farm for the reading of the will. They were desperate to know who had got the prize-winning flock of Herdwick sheep. The lawyer explained how the sheep were to be divided – the eldest receiving half the flock, the middle brother a third, and the youngest a ninth.

The eldest brother asked the youngest to run out to the meadow and count the sheep. He returned to say there were seventeen.

The three brothers were quite good at sums, but they were mystified: seventeen sheep don't divide into halves, thirds or ninths! They needed help. They knew that in the village was a wise woman. They called her the hen-wife because she lived by herself and kept hens. She might be able to help.

The brothers raced to the hen-wife's cottage and knocked on the door. On entering, they found the hen-wife sitting in the corner with a large white hen on her lap. She stroked her chin, stating her sadness at the news of their father's death.

The brothers explained the problem of the seventeen sheep. The hen-wife told them that in the shed, at the back of the house, she had an old, black ram. She advised that if they took the ram back to their meadow, the sums would all work out.

She then made things more puzzling by saying she needed the ram back at the end of the day.

Confused, the brothers discussed the problem and, reassuring each other that she was the wise woman, they put a rope around the ram's neck and led it back to the meadow and the sheep their father had left them, making a total of eighteen.

The oldest brother knew he was entitled to half, i.e. nine; the middle brother knew he was entitled to a third, i.e. six; and the youngest brother knew he was entitled to a ninth, i.e. two.

Adding this together, nine, six and two equalled … seventeen, so they could return the ram.

They led the ram back, still puzzling over why they hadn't been able to divide them when they'd just had the seventeen sheep.

She was indeed the wise woman.

That night the three brothers invited her to join them in celebrating their father's life.

The King
& the
Storyteller

The story that follows was told to me by my friend Stephen Fellowes at our annual 'Tales in Trust' storytelling weekend. As my favourite way to open a story begins 'It wasn't in my time, it wasn't in your time, it was in a time when birds built their nests in old mens' beards', I really enjoy the pictures this story conjures up.

The ageing storyteller had wisdom and knowledge even greater than his long, white beard; a beard that could have comfortably nested a sizeable flock of sparrows. He was a master of riddles and magical tales, but sadly as advancing years and infirmity started to overtake him, some of the magic faded. While he wasn't exactly losing it, he just wasn't quite as sharp. Most of his audiences still delighted in the wonder of his fairy tales and ghost stories as he slowly replaced memory with experience and imagination. This was not good enough, however, to satisfy his toughest audience: the young king of the land. He needed his storytelling performances to be sharper and with more edge than the old sage was capable of delivering. In short, the young king was becoming bored with the old man. When an arrogant young king is bored, that means trouble. In those days it probably meant that it wouldn't be long before you met the executioner.

The wise old storyteller, however, was far from finished and had a cunning plan to secure his stay of execution. He told the king, who arrogantly believed he could answer every riddle in the world, that he would ask him a riddle that he would never solve. He wisely secured the promise that he could never be sent to his death unless the king could answer the riddle correctly. This challenge hooked the king, who demanded to be told the riddle. Standing before the king's throne while stroking his long white beard, the sage uttered the riddle:

I can take you on a journey,
Without wings, wheels or sails,
And you may travel better with your eyes
    closed.
What am I ?

The young king thought hard until his brow furrowed. He had no idea of the answer. He dispatched the old storyteller to the dungeon as the executioner sharpened his sword in expectation.

Time seemed to pass slowly for the old storyteller until one day the king summoned the storyteller up from the dungeon. He commanded the old man to tell him the riddle one more time. Delighted to realise the king had not yet worked out the answer, stroking his beard he said:

I can take you on a journey,
Without wings wheels or sails,
And you may travel better with your eyes
    closed.
What am I?

The king seemed even more frustrated and grumpy than the last time, and he again dispatched his nemesis to the dungeon as the executioner once again sharpened his sword in expectation.

The days became weeks, the weeks became months and the months even became years. Then one day the old man was again summoned up from the dungeon, but this time he was led to the king's bedchamber. When he was taken in he saw that the king, dangerously ill from a wound sustained in battle, was lying propped up on the pillows of his bed. The king, who was only able to speak in a whisper, told the storyteller to draw nearer so that he could speak to him. The storyteller realised that the king was dying. As he drew close to the king, the king asked him to repeat the riddle one last time as it had irked him that he had never been able to solve it. It was unfinished business. The only thing that would be worse for the king than requesting the answer, would be dying without knowing it. Respectfully the storyteller said:

> I can take you on a journey,
> Without wings wheels or sails,
> And you may travel better with your eyes
>   closed.
> What am I ?

The king asked the bearded sage to reveal the answer while he still had life.

The storyteller quietly told him the answer and the king nodded and smiled in the knowledge that he had been outwitted. Just before he drew his last breath the king ordered that the storyteller be released in order to continue his important work of passing on the stories and riddles.

Now the king of course was dying! To find out the answer to the riddle, but to save you this fate, you can find it on the answers page. If you haven't already solved it.

ANSWERS

Riddles Good Enough to Eat

1 Chilli.
2 Cherry.
3 Strawberry.
4 Sweetcorn.
5 Egg.
6 Swallow.

In the Garden Riddles Grow

1 Sunflower.
2 Elder tree (first you get elderflower
   champagne and later you get elderberry
   wine).
3 Rowan tree.
4 Leaf.
5 Catkin.
6 Harebells.

Racing for the Crown

The two words were 'swap horses'.

Four Pairs of Shorts

1   The answer he gave was 'man', you & I.
      In the morning of our life we get around on all fours,
      In the afternoon of our lives we use two legs,
      In the evening of our lives we use a walking stick.

2   The beggar was a girl.

3   It was a grandfather, father (son) and son
    (grandson).

4   Louise, for she styled the hair of Poppy
    (she also does this storyteller's hair!).

5   Friday was the name of his horse.

6   'An apple a day keeps the doctor away!'

7   In a cowshed a man sat on a three-legged
    stool eating a chicken leg. A dog came in
    and snatched the chicken leg. The man
    stood up and threw the stool at the dog,
    who dropped the chicken leg in a cow pat.

8   John is a man's name and the dentist, the
    doctor and the lawyer were all women.

A Riddle Gallimaufry

1   Spectacles.
2   Pencil.
3   Sailing ship.
4   Violin.
5   Boots.
6   Coffin.

Riddles Grow Out of the Land

1   River.
2   Snowflake.
3   Desert.
4   Horizon.
5   Map.
6   Sand.
7   The wind.

The King and the Storyteller

The answer to the old storyteller's riddle is
'a story'.

And Finally...

When I first appear I am mysterious
But once revealed, I am not serious.
What am I?

If you can solve this one you have indeed
completed our riddle journey.
If not, just turn this page.

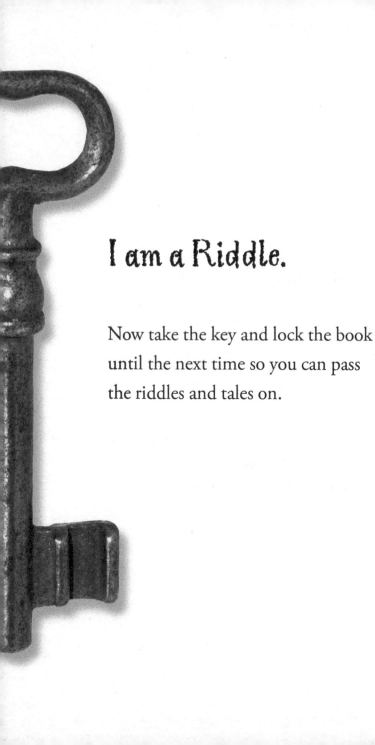

I am a Riddle.

Now take the key and lock the book until the next time so you can pass the riddles and tales on.